Mop Hop

Consultants

Ashley Bishop, Ed.D.
Sue Bishop, M.E.D.

Publishing Credits

Dona Herweck Rice, *Editor-in-Chief*
Robin Erickson, *Production Director*
Lee Aucoin, *Creative Director*
Tim J. Bradley, *Illustrator Manager*
Jason Peltz, *Illustrator*
Sharon Coan, *Project Manager*
Jamey Acosta, *Editor*
Rachelle Cracchiolo, M.A.Ed., *Publisher*

Teacher Created Materials

5301 Oceanus Drive
Huntington Beach, CA 92649-1030
http://www.tcmpub.com
ISBN 978-1-4333-2933-3
© 2012 Teacher Created Materials, Inc.
Printed in China WAI002

mop

I can mop.

hop

I can hop.

bop

I can bop.

top

I am on top!

I need a pop!

Glossary

Sight Words

I can
an on
need a

Extension Activities

Read the story together with your child. Use the discussion questions before, during, and after your reading to deepen your child's understanding of the story and the rime (word family) that is introduced.

The activities provide fun ideas for continuing the conversation about the story and the vocabulary that is introduced. They will help your child make personal connections to the story and use the vocabulary to describe prior experiences.

Discussion Questions
- What is the girl in the story standing on top of?
- Why do we need to mop? Have you ever mopped a kitchen floor?
- Have you ever seen a mouse? What did you do?
- What is your favorite popsicle flavor?

Activities at Home
- Review the *-op* words in the story. Work with your child to act them out and discuss their definitions. Talk with your child about synonyms for each *-op* word.
- Talk about how people are often afraid of mice. Ask your child to share what makes him or her scared. Have your child act out what happens when something surprising or frightening occurs.